COCK-A-
DOODLE-DOO!

Published by Prion Books
20 Mortimer Street
London W1T 3JW

Images copyright © 2007 Ross Adams
Layout and design copyright © 2012
Carlton Books Limited

ISBN 978-1-78097-033-2

10 9 8 7 6 5 4 3 2

Printed in China

The material in this book was previously
published in *Dirty Doodles*

Thank you: miss boakes, luke + roland, the family, parker, lamy, normal and you.

COCK-A-DOODLE-DOO!

Rose Adders

CARLTON

Draw in this book

Colour in the images

Fill in the drawings

Stick things in it

Fill the pages with emotions

Cover the pages in liquid

Punish the pages – they've been naughty!

It's your book . . . use it!

Who's blocking YOUR sun?

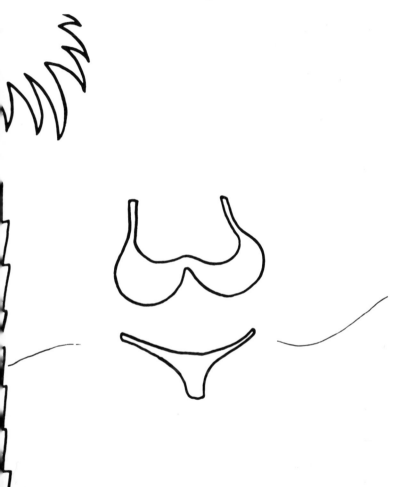

What could you measure?

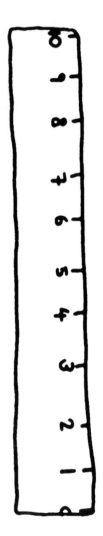

Is this something you didn't know about your parents?

What could these be?

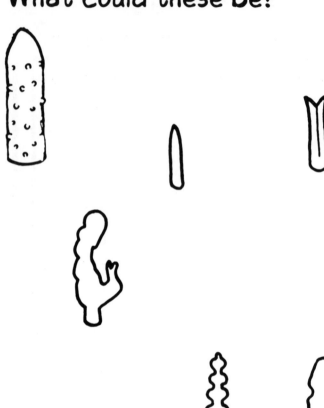

What are you spying on?

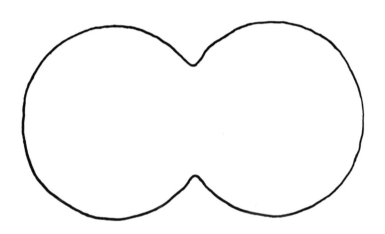

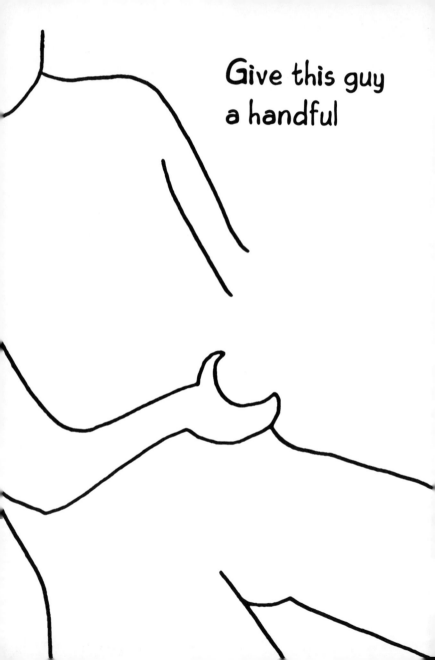

Give this guy
a handful

Make an animal from this

Nice shoes!

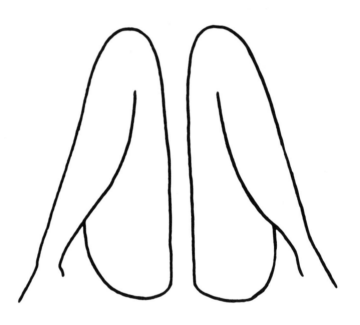

Finish the flasher

Get the cock to
the crackers...

Lines and lines and lines
and lines and lines...

Journey to the centre of...

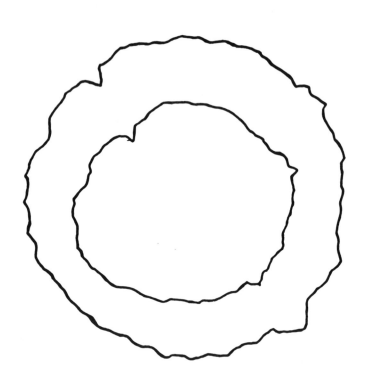

Alien eyes or funny fruit?

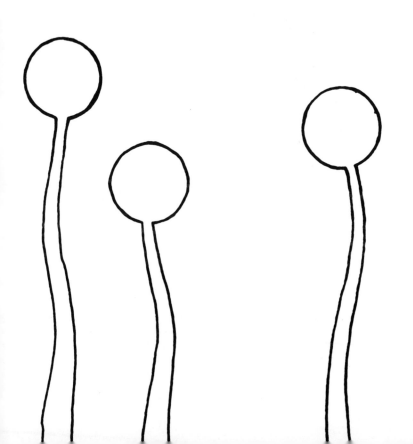

From a different dimension

Eeeeeeeeeee splat!

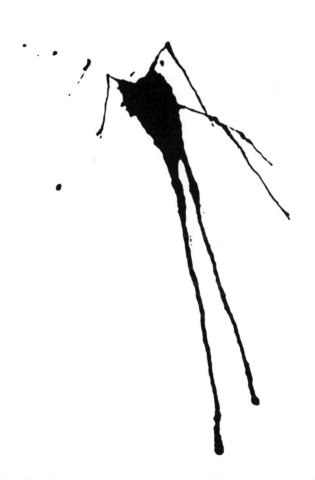

What's popped out of the magic hat?

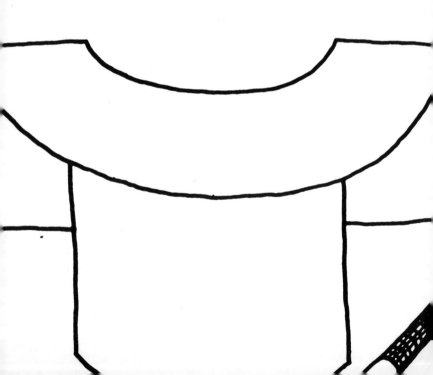

Draw your queen

Make your own jigsaw

Is that a pistol in your fist?

What's this wobbly roundshape?

Where was the chopper dropped?

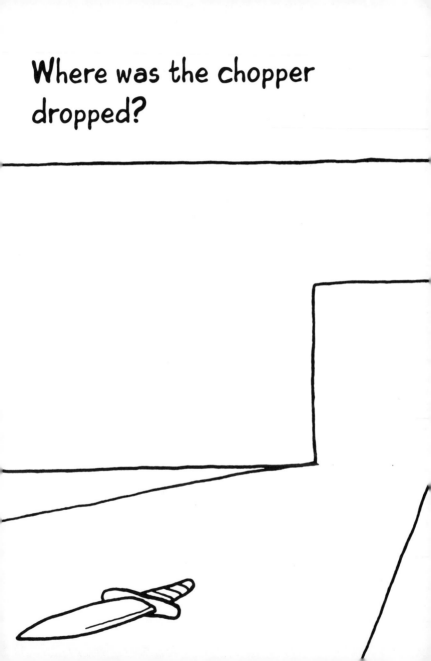

Complete the pointy instrument

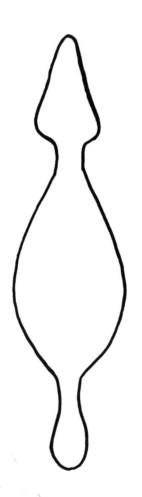

Make your own stamp

Udder dog or cat's bum?

What's going on in this bed?

What do you think is
dangling overhead?

What sort of creature is this?

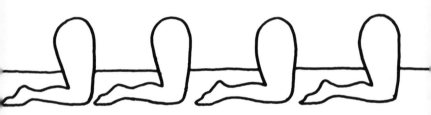

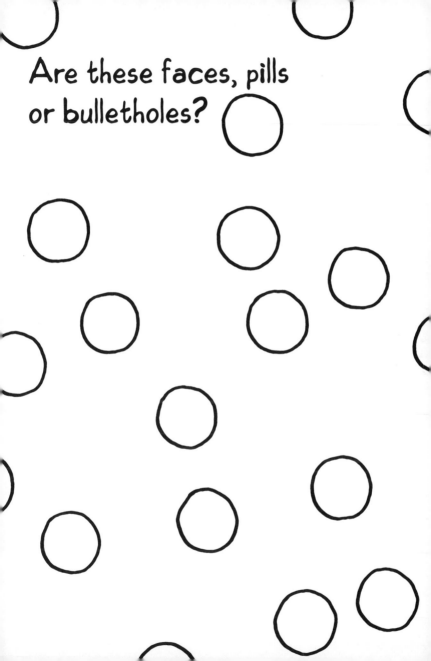

Are these faces, pills or bulletholes?

Are you off your trolley?

What's your sign?

Give the skeleton a bone?

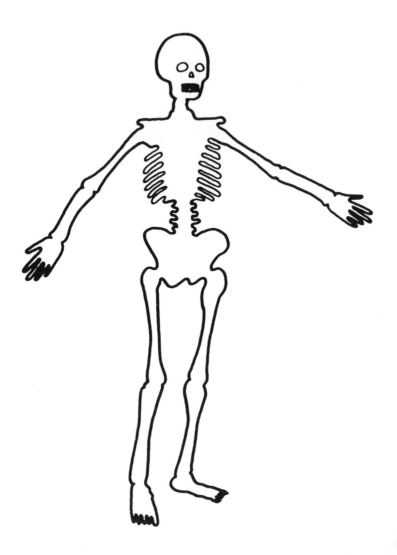

What's in the boot?

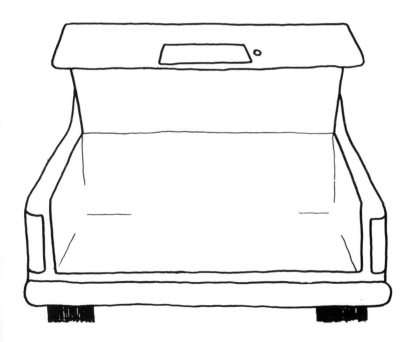

Half-man, half-?

What could these be?

Twins?

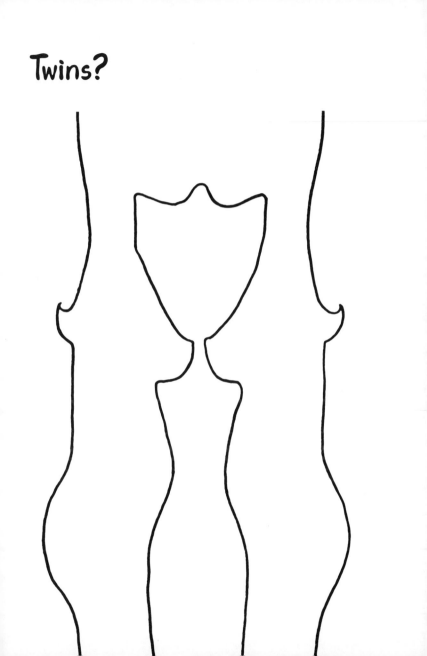

Can you make something out of this?

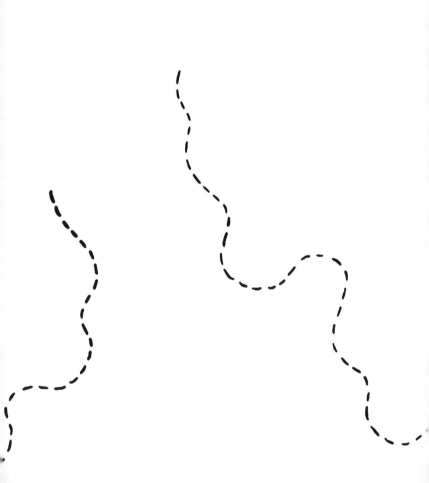

It's a wabbit!

Where does food come from?

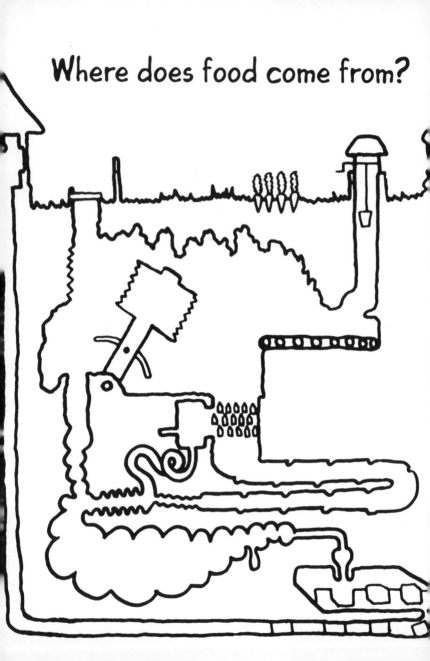

What's this little birdie saying?

What's packed like sardines?

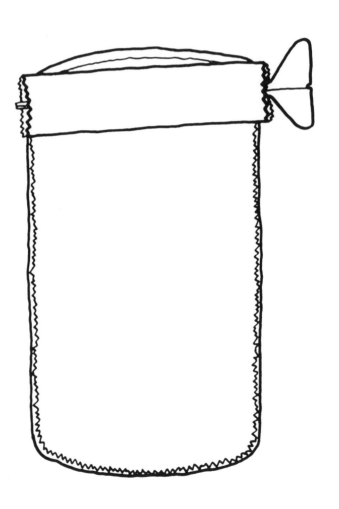

Who the hell is that?

Silhouettes...

Hey, ugly dude

Give the horse a magical horn

Draw your old school wall

Life drawing class

What's on the operating table?

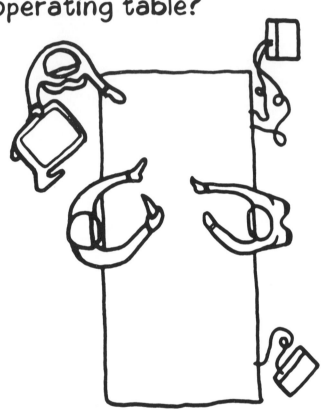

Something under the table?

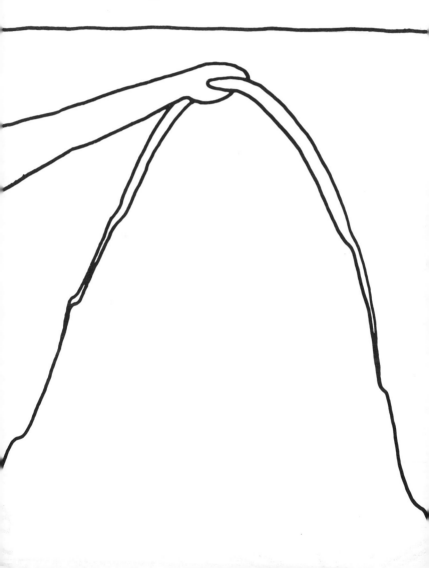

Who's chewing on the new sweety bar?

Tumblers!

Complete the toolbox

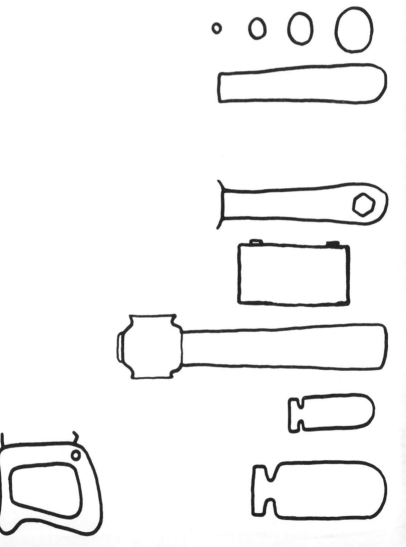

What else has been sucked up?

Who's the dogsbody?

You found an old polaroid

What's been left in the rock star's dressing room?

Hang out your dirty washing

Who's hanging out in the park?

Have fun on the slippery slide

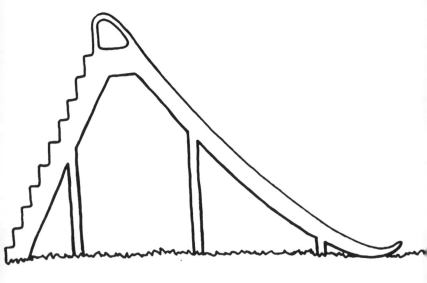

Draw the shadows

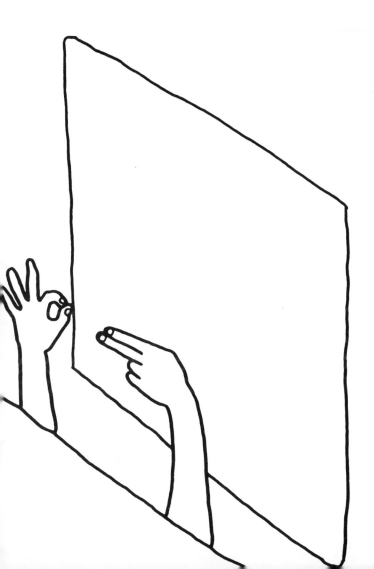

Save Dave!

Dave needs a relaxing seat

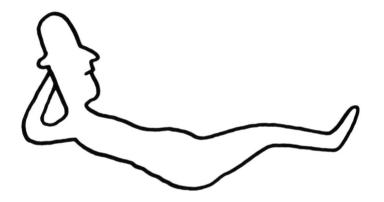

What has grown wings?

Finish off the exotic dancers

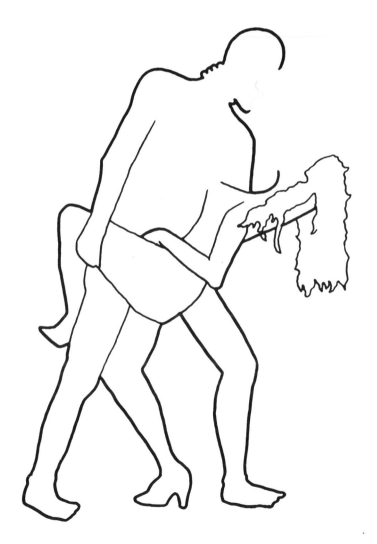

What's the frog catching?

Scary shouting old baglady!

Who's in nappies?

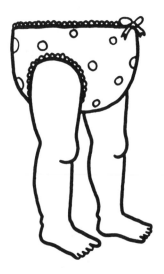

Eurgh!

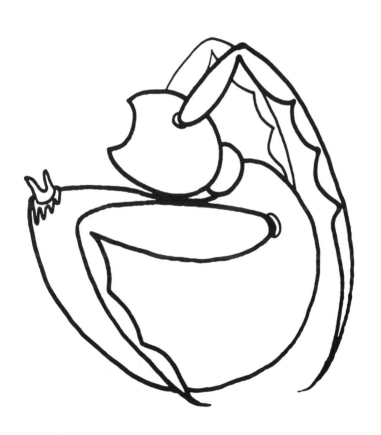

You will obey!

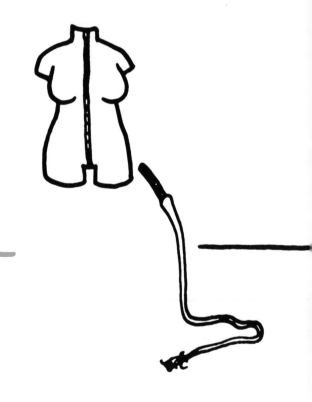

Cut something

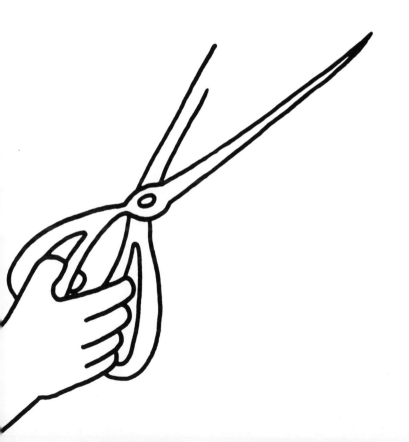

What is Dave up to?

Ug, my brain hurts

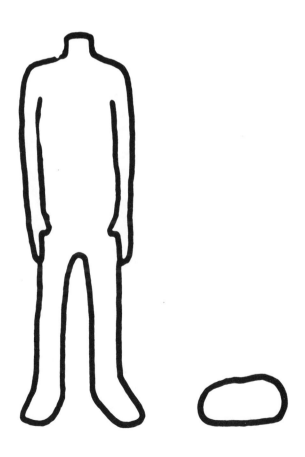

Help fatty perform the Nutcracker

Is that a Mexican hat?

Who's in chains?

What is Dave riding?

Who's in the red light window?

Fill the fruit bowl

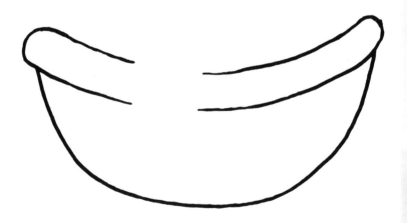

What's in the case?

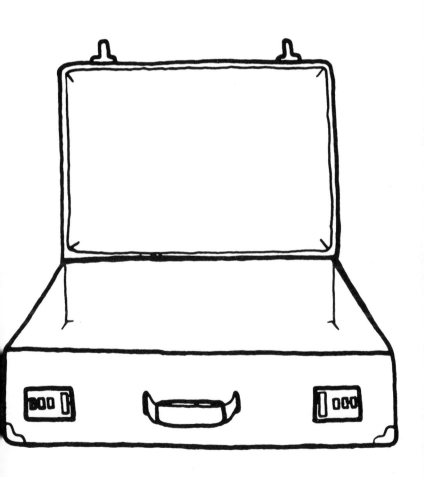

What's swinging in the park?

Draw your own
cartoon character

Sew the head back
on your favourite teddy

What are these?

Draw your own customized personal stereo

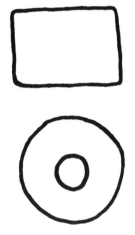

Join the dots?

What's this?

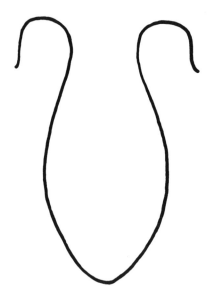

Is there something inside?

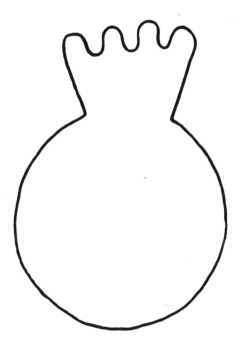

Draw a big balloon ride